SEA AUSTRALIA

WITH STEVE PARISH

Steve Parish

PUBLISHING

FOR JAN

Have you ever felt wet sand between your toes?

Ever felt the sting of sun on hot skin
while breathing in
the sweet smell of salty air?

Ever walked with someone –
talking, touching,
playing in the sun?

Ever shared the past, the now, the future,
talked and laughed and shared your inner feelings?

I have.

I've jumped the tide-line,
watched the bird-line
with a very special someone.

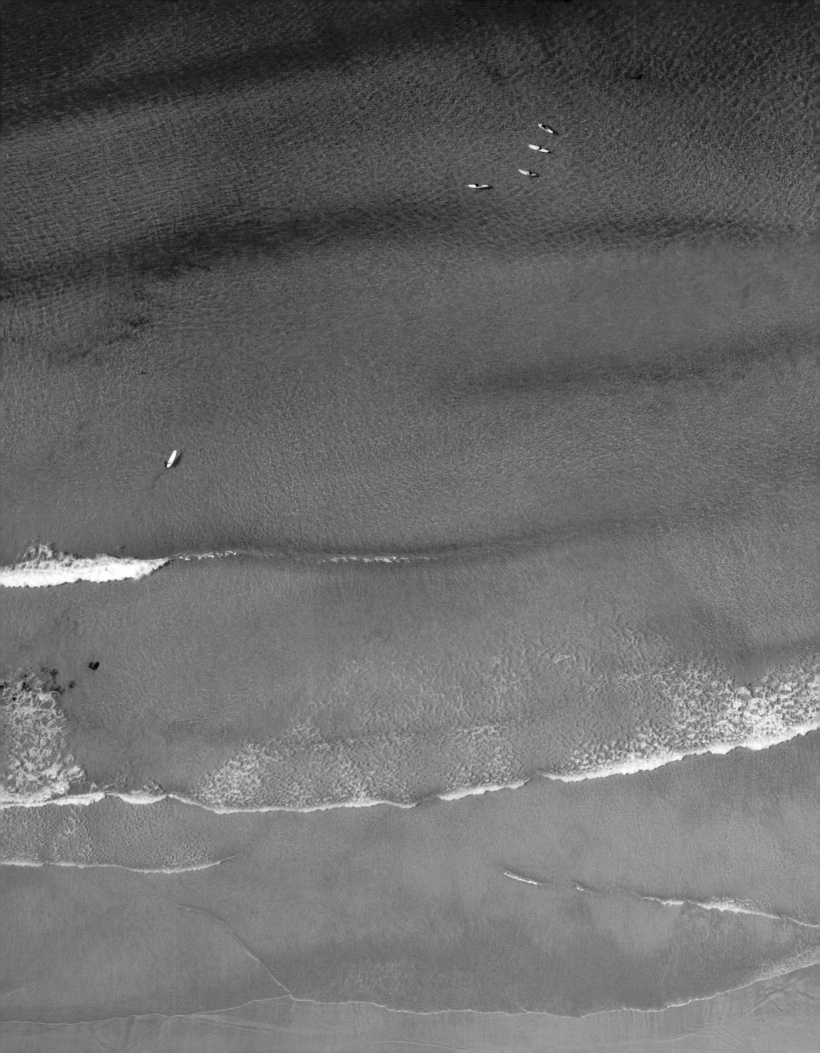

SEA
AUSTRALIA

WITH STEVE PARISH

Steve Parish
PUBLISHING

SPONSORED BY.

water

ON SEA

My earliest memories of the sea focus on its constant movement. As a small child, I stared in wonder as shimmering expanses of water lifted into silver crests, raced landwards, bowed in front of me and swirled gifts of foam, bright shells and stranded weed around my skinny, sunburned legs.

At eighteen, I went to sea on a warship. For twelve seemingly endless months we steamed from Australia to Japan, to China, Malaysia and Indonesia before turning homewards again. Twelve months of staring at the too-blue horizon, at a world of boats and the faces of people who live on the sea engraved the magic power of the ocean on my soul.

Today, the sea remains my refuge, my haven and my enchanted world.

There are many who share my passion. Time spent on, or by, or in, the ocean is savoured, then relived in memories and dreams. Our bodies may be on land, carrying out the tasks of everyday, but our souls remain at sea.

BESIDE SEA

Once, there was no sea on Earth. Then water from the sky fell upon the molten land and filled its hollows with coolness and became a first home for living creatures. So the sea is very ancient and its magic is very powerful.

Walk by the sea and you will sense this magic. On a warm, twilit evening, the shell-ground sands of a coral cay will whisper underfoot, casting spells of unwinding and sensuality. At dawn, the wave-cut platforms of more temperate shores will provide places to stand and contemplate life's endless possibilities.

I have walked, talked and found friendship and inspiration over many a seaside kilometre.

CORAL CAY REFLECTIONS

REFLECTIONS FROM A ROCK PLATFORM

MANFISH

UNDER SEA

Few land habitats – perhaps only the most exotic of rainforests – equal the biodiversity and richness of life around an ocean reef. The diver is immersed in animal and plant life, swims in a living soup of microscopic organisms, is surrounded by some of the loveliest and most remarkable of the planet's creatures.

I believe that scuba-diving, perfectly weighted so that my body floats without effort, is the perfect, relaxing, back-to-the-womb flotation experience. A gentle flipper movement and I glide forwards, or upwards, or downwards. A slight twist of my torso and I discover that the almost imperceptible pressure change I sensed around me was caused by a huge grouper which hangs in the blue, fins twisting lazily as it studies me. Perhaps it is thinking, "What a fine specimen of surface life!" and will tick me off in its humanwatcher's notebook.

This is my favourite foreign country, where I hope my visitor's visa will always be renewed.

MAKING A DISCOVERY

DESERT COAST, FRANCOIS PERON NATIONAL PARK, WESTERN AUSTRALIA

SEA AUSTRALIA • THE JOURNEY

I remember very clearly Christmas Day the year I was nine. We were taking our annual family holiday at Moana Beach, just south of Adelaide, and I had sneaked to the Christmas tree very early in the morning to see how many goodies were labelled STEPHEN. The first present I fondled felt lumpy and strange, and I spent some time anxiously trying to identify the contents by touch through the festive paper. Three long hours later, I was allowed to unwrap a face mask and a snorkel – items which would open up a road I would follow for the rest of my life.

The next huge step on that road was the day I took my first photograph underwater. I was 16 years old and I had been invited to take part in a South Australian Museum fish collection expedition to Kangaroo Island, just off the coast of South Australia. While diving, I was handed an underwater camera to try my hand at focusing, and exposed a single frame. Six weeks later at a reunion the photograph was screened for all to see and applaud. I had actually managed to get the fish in focus (not easy in gloomy, dark water) and I was hooked!

I am not unique in my passion for the sea. Australia's nearly 37 000-kilometre, for the most part accessible, coastline offers explorers, fishermen, holidaymakers, surfers, divers, sailors and just sea-lovers enormous variety. From the northern tip of Cape York to South East Cape in Tasmania, from the eastern extremity of Cape Byron to the West's Steep Point and all coastal points in between, there are multitudinous coastlines, each with its unique seascapes, flora and fauna.

The images in this book, only a tiny number of the many, many thousands exposed on my 35-year journey, represent some of the reasons why Australians are obsessed with their ocean. The pictures have been selected in an attempt to bring together a sea-taste of events and encounters which will, I trust, stimulate, excite and entertain you.

Steve Parish

CONTENTS

Sea Australia — an introduction.................... 13

Queensland 16

New South Wales 82

Victoria 140

Tasmania 176

South Australia 186

Western Australia 214

Northern Territory 246

A plea for sea...............................258

AZURE SKY, SAPPHIRE SEA AND SILVER SAILS ON A SUNDRENCHED QUEENSLAND SUMMER DAY

QUEENSLAND

The Sunshine State has 2500 kilometres of coastline which offer a wide variety of spectacular scenery.

From the mangrove forests and mudflats of the Gulf of Carpentaria to the tip of Cape York, and southward again to Cairns, the adventurer will experience some of the world's most exciting wilderness inlets and estuaries. Here are sand dunes, stark rocky headlands and rainforests. South again is the magnificent Central Queensland coast, terminating in the delights of the Whitsundays, then the natural and human wonders of the Sunshine and Gold Coasts and the splendid sand islands of the State's southeastern corner.

Now go into sensory overload and add the fabulous, fantastic, fascinating Great Barrier Reef!

Colour coastal Queensland brilliant blue and gold, and join me as I savour its delectable delights.

ON A TYPICAL QUEENSLAND BEACH

THURSDAY ISLAND LIES OFF THE TIP OF CAPE YORK

There is a strange Australian mania for leaping into a four-wheel-drive vehicle, battling in the shortest time to a faraway place, taking hasty souvenir photos, then hurrying home. During the dry months of the year, satellite images probably show one long stream of dust marking the trail travellers leave behind as they hurtle northwards to Cape York, congratulate each other, then rush south again.

Go to Cape York. Take your time. Look around on the way. And when you get there, go to Thursday Island as well.

THE TOP OF AUSTRALIA, CAPE YORK

A FEMALE FLATBACK TURTLE PREPARES TO LAY HER EGGS

THE EASTERN ASPECT OF FAR CAPE YORK PENINSULA

The coast of Cape York Peninsula offers some of the finest dune systems, tropical heathlands, sand and mud coastal habitats and all-round wilderness to be seen anywhere in the world. Amongst other rare fauna, the Flatback Turtle, which is found only in Australia, may be seen coming ashore to lay eggs between November and January. Sea turtles are increasingly endangered, and watching one of these marine marvels in this most intimate moment is a privilege to be treasured and placed amongst the great memories of a lifetime.

A VERY LARGE ADULT SALTWATER CROCODILE

On one expedition in search of turtles, we landed on a small island 25 kilometres out to sea. We walked the beach searching for turtle traces; then, returning to the boat, we discovered nearby the tracks of a huge Saltwater Crocodile. Obviously we had not noticed as it slept very near our mooring point. "Salties" abound on tropical coasts, usually living along rivers and estuaries and amongst mangroves, but some adventuresome individuals do take to sea. We were quite happy that our long-toothed voyager had chosen to avoid a meeting.

CAPE FLATTERY NATIONAL PARK

A GREEN TURTLE COMES ASHORE TO LAY HER EGGS ON RAINE ISLAND

SAND FLIES AS THE TURTLE DIGS A PIT TO FIT HER BULKY BODY

LEDGES LIKE THIS MAY EITHER TRAP OR UPTURN TURTLES. THE TOWER WAS BUILT BY CONVICTS

Raine Island, at the northern end of the Great Barrier Reef, is quite unlike any other coral cay. It is dominated by a convict-built watchtower and supports one of the world's largest breeding colonies of Green Turtles. Life is tough on Raine Island. So is death. The huge numbers of turtles jostling for a place on its inhospitable shores means that during peak breeding season there is a constant procession of armour-bound creatures seeking nest sites. Many lose their way in the coral rocks, jam themselves under ledges or simply become exhausted in the fierce midday sun. Their bleached remains are reminders that in tropical seas only the fittest, and the luckiest, survive.

PHOTOGRAPHING BENEATH THE CORAL SEA

EXAMINING A GIANT CORAL SEA FAN

The northern extremity of the Reef and its extensions westwards into the Coral Sea are wonderworlds of marine life. To have the freedom of these waters on a clear, calm day is the culmination of any diver's wildest dreams. Giant coral sea fans, manta rays, giant grouper, reef sharks, fish in bewildering shapes, sizes and colours – it's an underwater fantasy carried to extremes, a place no-one would believe existed without photographic evidence.

A TRIO OF ELEGANT LONG-FINNED BANNERFISH

Photographing reef fish has been a challenge I have met head-on and with enthusiasm for over 35 years. Nowhere is making portraits of the ocean's beauties more challenging than on the Great Barrier Reef and in adjacent Coral Sea waters. Here, in a world of coral labyrinths and surrounded by abundant food, thousands of species abound. Some swim around the diver boldly, others are extremely timid. Others still are rarely seen by day and may only be captured on film successfully at night.

EMPEROR ANGELFISH

GOLDEN DAMSELFISH

LIZARD ISLAND, A CONTINENTAL ISLAND AND A NATIONAL PARK

COOKTOWN, NEAREST PORT TO LIZARD ISLAND

A CORAL-FILLED LAGOON FRINGING LIZARD ISLAND

Lizard Island is Queensland's most northerly resort island, a rocky cut-off piece of the mainland surrounded by coral reefs. Like many others, I have sweated in the steps of Captain Cook, who in 1770 climbed with naturalist Joseph Banks to the island's summit. After anxious searching of the reef mazes that stretched before them, they sighted a narrow channel through which their barque *Endeavour* could escape the coral prison which surrounded her. I have also admired the large but wary monitor lizards which gave this spectacular island its name.

MANGROVES ON THE OLIVER CREEK WALK, CAPE TRIBULATION NATIONAL PARK

Along the shores of Cape Tribulation National Park the rainforest mingles with mangroves, those wondrous trees which endure daily cycles of saltwater submersion and aerial exposure. Beside Oliver Creek runs an 800-metre boardwalk which gives entry to a world where pop-eyed fish climb out on tree roots, crabs are coloured like butterflies and brilliant birds light almost within arm's reach and serenade the watcher with song. In the mangroves, the quiet watcher can sense what life in a primeval swamp must have been like.

I admit I am not a hero. I do *not* enjoy sinking knee-deep in mud while tripping over shell-encrusted mangrove roots and fighting off the unwelcome attentions of hordes of biting insects. That little weakness in my character is why I adore Cape Tribulation National Park.

Here gorgeous mangrove trees grow in firm sand over which flows crystal-clear water, and where I can photograph at sunset and at sunrise without being carried away and carved up for dinner, or drained of precious body fluids, by tiny winged predators.

CAPE TRIBULATION NATIONAL PARK

THE MOUTH OF THE DAINTREE RIVER

The march of the rainforest-clad mountains right down to the sparkling sea in Cape Tribulation National Park, between the mouth of the Daintree River and Cooktown, gives rise to a phenomenon which never fails to thrill and excite me. At dawn the mountains act as giant sound reflectors. If you are fortunate enough to be wandering the tideline as the horizon pales and the sun rises, the sounds of a tropical rainforest farewelling the night and greeting the day are unforgettable. Birds, bats, insects, water sources sing – I swear that even the leaves on the trees and the fungi on their trunks contribute their own rustlings and squeakings and chirpings to the symphony.

I return time after time to the challenge of capturing on film the area's tremendous and sudden changes as tropical storms and calms flicker across its magnificent tropical vistas.

There has been much controversy about the preservation of this unique area, particularly since 1981 when Cape Tribulation National Park was declared. Areas of the lowland tropical rainforest have since been cleared, an action which to my mind is not only criminal but incomprehensible.

THE LOW ISLES ARE 63 KILOMETRES NORTH OF CAIRNS

CAIRNS, TOURIST CAPITAL OF NORTH QUEENSLAND

Cairns always seems to me a city with two faces. One is the non-stop international play-centre, where jet planes deliver overseas visitors to savour the delights of Reef, rainforest and mountains. This Cairns features superb restaurants, top hotels and a glossy facade. The other Cairns lives at a slower pace, and is a place of traditional high-set houses, lovingly tended and luxurious gardens, warm, homely hospitality and some of the best chances to enjoy nature you'll find in Australia.

GREEN ISLAND, 27 KILOMETRES NORTHEAST OF CAIRNS, HAS AN UNDERWATER OBSERVATORY

Near Cairns, the Great Barrier Reef lies closer to the mainland than anywhere further south, and the Low Isles and Green Island are only two of the coral cays easily visited on day trips. I have a double fascination with viewing these cays from the air. My mind appreciates the way in which tiny, soft coral creatures have built their castles of stone from the ocean floor. My soul revels in the abstract patterns and brilliant colours of deeps, shallows, channels and coral enclaves.

THE CAIRNS MUDFLAT, A HAVEN FOR WADERS AND SEABIRDS

HINCHINBROOK ISLAND NATIONAL PARK

PART OF HINCHINBROOK ISLAND'S MAGNIFICENT EASTERN ASPECT

THE NORTHWESTERN COASTLINE OF HINCHINBROOK ISLAND

Hinchinbrook Island combines two of my ruling passions. It is a place of scenic beauty surrounded by sea, and it is a National Park. It may well be the world's largest island National Park and it certainly boasts one of Australia's finest walking tracks, extending from Cape Richards to Mulligan Bay. Splendid birding, especially in the mangroves on the western side, wonderful marine life, glorious beaches, superb fishing and sailing – who could ask for more?

WHITSUNDAY ISLAND AT SUNSET, A WONDERFUL WILDERNESS SCENE

A QUIET WHITSUNDAY BACKWATER AT DAWN

AIRLIE BEACH, GATEWAY TO THE WHITSUNDAY ISLANDS

Airlie Beach is the gateway to the Whitsunday Islands, an area that rivals any coastal seascape in the world for scenic beauty. This blue-green necklace of islands offers boating adventures and opportunities for sheer, self-indulgent, unadulterated relaxation, whether in the form of a luxury holiday on Hayman, Hamilton, Daydream or Hook Islands, or a more self-sufficient period, either ashore or on board one of many charter boats.

SAILING AND BOATING THE WHITSUNDAY ISLANDS

Every sailor knows the sense of contentment that rules when safe anchorage is reached, gear is stowed and the voyagers are free to swim, fish, do chores or simply relax. Pentecost Island (top right) and Whitehaven Beach (bottom left) are two fine Whitsunday anchorages.

EACH BOAT IS A WORLD TO ITSELF, BUT ALL SAILORS ARE UNITED IN THE LOVE OF VOYAGING

DRIFTING MANGROVE LEAVES, HILL INLET, WHITSUNDAY ISLAND

TOP LEFT AND CLOCKWISE: SCENES IN THE WHITSUNDAY GROUP:
NARA INLET; PENTECOST ISLAND; HILL INLET; CID HARBOUR

One of the joys the sea brings to me is the contrast between its grand scenes and its intimate glimpses. Flying over a coastline, I admire the miniaturisation of rugged mountains, sapphire bays and darker-blue channels. Wandering the tideline, I look for smaller but no less moving visual treats – hermit crab tracks stencilled in sand, a nautilus shell stranded in splendour, or a burnished drift of mangrove leaves swaying in the turn-of-tide ripples.

MAGNETIC ISLAND IS KNOWN FOR UNSPOILED BEACHES

Eight kilometres from busy Townsville, and easily accessible by fast ferry, rugged Magnetic Island is a haven for holidaymakers and a very desirable residential address – though only around 2000 happy people have the latter privilege. This is a getaway island for families and tourists alike, with fine beaches, fringing reefs, and walking tracks which offer spectacular views.

TOWER HILL GUARDS THE THRIVING CITY OF TOWNSVILLE

The brooding granite hulk of Tower Hill looms over Townsville, a port which was established in the 1860s and which contains some gems of Queensland's distinctive Victorian architecture. A centre for marine and tropical research, Townsville offers a magnificent Environmental Park, is base for a variety of island cruises and some topline scuba-diving experiences, and enjoys sunshine for around 282 days every year.

MASTHEAD ISLAND IS PART OF THE CAPRICORN-BUNKER GROUP OF ISLANDS

TINY ERSKINE ISLAND

Having spent the first 30 years of my life diving in dark southern seas, I expected nothing different from the waters of the Great Barrier Reef. On my first voyage to these northern reefs, the vessel left Gladstone at night and travelled east to Wistari Reef, part of the Capricorn-Bunker group of islands. At sunrise, I climbed from my bunk and rushed to the gunwhale. Peering over, I felt as if I had been hit in the chest. I literally gasped for breath, such was the the impact of the multitudinous shoals and schools of fish swimming in the clear water below. Minutes later, I had my camera and was over the side. I was amazed to discover that the sea floor, which had appeared only a few metres below the surface, in fact lay beneath 20 metres of crystalline water.

LADY MUSGRAVE ISLAND, AT THE LOWER END OF THE CAPRICORN-BUNKER GROUP

A DIVE BOAT HEADS OUT FROM HERON ISLAND

THE MOMENT ALL HAVE BEEN WAITING FOR

Divers are drawn from all parts of the world to explore the clear, calm waters of the Great Barrier Reef. In the southern part of the Reef, Heron and Lady Elliot Islands are popular destinations. The Heron Island Bommie, a huge head of coral, is a particular heaven for divers. Here, large fish have become accustomed to human intrusion in their home and provide a living marine Mardi Gras of brilliant colours, fantastic shapes and swirling, graceful, swift-finned movement.

WATCHING ANEMONE FISh RESTING IN THEIR ANEMONE HOME

EXPLORING A REEF FLAT, HERON ISLAND

It is easy to become caught up in the thrills of underwater investigation and to forget that the reef flats also offer a wonderful opportunity to meet sea creatures at a different level. In fact, exploring the reef flats demands a high level of sensitivity and thoughtfulness from the human investigator, as corals are fragile and break easily under the weight of the over-eager. Wading, using a clear-bottomed viewing box and snorkelling are ways to participate in the intertidal universe of corals, sea stars, molluscs and multi coloured fish.

TOP LEFT AND CLOCKWISE: MOORISH IDOL; PINNATE BATFISH;
ORANGE-FIN ANEMONE FISH; CORAL COD

Fish-watching can become as much of an obsession as birdwatching. In fact, it is far easier than birdwatching (apart from the difficulties of consulting a field guide underwater), because many fish simply ignore the diver as they go about their daily preoccupations of eating and avoiding being eaten. I am constantly lost in wonder at the intricate jigsaw which is fish society, in which each species slots neatly into its own part of the puzzle, finding living space and food in ways which are uniquely its own.

BEAKED CORAL FISH

A SCHOOL OF BIGEYE TREVALLY

As I slip into the sea, I leave my land-based cares behind me. My body goes on full alert, sensing any change in the water around me, appreciating the textures and positions of coral and rocks, watching the myriads of underwater creatures which live out their busy lives between surface and sea floor.

THE MANTA RAY, ONE OF THE MOST MAJESTIC OF SEA CREATURES

SCHOOLING FISH BECOME EXOTIC SHAPES AGAINST SURFACE SPARKLE AND SUN

MASKED GANNET AND DOWNY CHICK, SWAINS REEF

WHAT BETTER WAY TO DISCOVER PHOTOGRAPHY?

Photography is easy and enjoyable. Just buy a camera and film, read the instructions carefully and go! go! go! However, I should warn you that seeing those first images captured on film may change your life forever. Gone will be the comfortable days of sitting in your car watching the waves. Instead, you will be out on the beach, wandering the tideline, camera at the ready, forever chasing that perfect picture.

A LOGGERHEAD TURTLE COMES ASHORE TO LAY HER EGGS

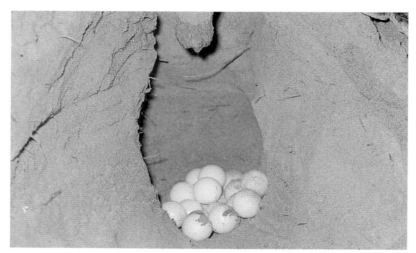

AROUND 120 SOFT, ROUND EGGS ARE LAID IN A PIT DUG IN SAND

SEVERAL MONTHS LATER, TURTLE HATCHLINGS ERUPT FROM THE SAND

FILMING A NATURE DOCUMENTARY: A LOGGERHEAD LAYING HER EGGS ON MON REPOS BEACH, 15 KILOMETRES NORTH OF BUNDABERG

I have watched many female turtles lay their eggs and, as the photo above shows, I am not alone in my fascination. The spectacle is a moving one for humans, but they should remember that successful egg-laying is vital to the survival of these endangered creatures. Spectators should remain quietly at a distance until laying has commenced, when the turtle will tolerate soft light and a few gentle touches. Hatchlings, which become disoriented by lights, should be left alone to make their hazardous way to the perils of the sea.

WHALE-WATCHING, HERVEY BAY

August, September and October each year find vessels full of eager whale-lovers chugging into southern Barrier Reef waters, eager to spot Humpback Whales on their annual migration. Hervey Bay, between Fraser Island and the mainland, is a stretch of calm water where mothers and calves relax and males compete with gigantic leapings and tail-splashings. To watch a boatload of quiet, reserved people turn into uninhibited fans who clutch each other and scream at the merest sighting of a spout or a tail, and fall about in a frenzy if a whale breaches, is to be reminded that wild creatures can arouse passions even deeper than those dragged from teenagers by rock bands.

HUMPBACKS AT HERVEY BAY

TAIL-SLAPPING

A MALE WILL SLAP HIS TAIL ON THE WATER TO INTIMIDATE OTHER MALES IN COMPETITION FOR THE RIGHT TO SWIM WITH A FEMALE

I have had the good fortune to swim with Humpback Whales off the coasts of Australia and elsewhere in the South Pacific. Their power is awesome. With three beats of its tremendous tail a whale can hurl its 40 tonnes into the air, falling back into the water with an impact that makes a nearby watcher's ears ring. Once, while diving ten kilometres off the Gold Coast, I looked down into the blue-black abyss and could just make out a huge shape, with a smaller one alongside, looming up towards me. I hung in saltwater space, forgetting to breathe, as mother and calf, circled by silvery dolphins, rose under me. Just as I thought I was to be butted out of her way, the whale swerved. Swept backwards by her wash, I was alone again in the sea, blinking back tears of wonder and loss.

SCIENTISTS NAMED THE HUMPBACK WHALE "MEGAPTERA", OR "GREAT-WING", REFERRING TO ITS ENORMOUS FLIPPERS

IT IS WORTH TRAVELLING THOUSANDS OF KILOMETRES TO SEE A HUMPBACK WHALE BREACHING

PLAYING AMONG THE DUNES ON FRASER ISLAND

A DINGO ON A FRASER ISLAND BEACH

SKY MEETS SEA, FRASER ISLAND

The major battle fought between conservationists and those who wished to extract the natural resources of Fraser Island brought this magnificent sand island, the most extensive in the world, to the attention of the public. Largely due to the efforts of the admirable and determined John Sinclair, the island is now listed by the National Estate as a World Heritage National Park. Fraser Island is 123 kilometres long and extends over 184 000 hectares. Its marvels include superb beaches, freshwater creeks running to the sea through stands of rainforest, perched lakes filled with crystal water, heathlands vibrant with birds and a wealth of wildlife, including pure-blooded and fearless Dingos.

REFLECTING AS THE SUN SETS OVER THE GLASSHOUSE MOUNTAINS

FISHING THE SUNSHINE COAST

The Sunshine Coast, between Noosa and Bribie Island, is a playground for holidaymakers. I enjoy the friendly towns, with their restaurants and markets, but my best memories are of long lazy days on the water or on the beach, of the unspoiled beauties of Cooloola National Park and of magic moments on Bribie, looking westward across Pumicestone Passage to enjoy the setting sun silhouetting the Glasshouse Mountains.

COLOURED SANDS AT COOLOOLA NATIONAL PARK

NOOSA, A POPULAR HOLIDAY RESORT

MOOLOOLABA, A SCENIC COASTAL CENTRE

A WHITE-BELLIED SEA-EAGLE CALLS FOR ITS MATE

AN OSPREY RETURNS TO ITS NEST

The sand islands of Moreton Bay are composed of material transported by the sea from the northern beaches of New South Wales. Two of these islands, Moreton and Stradbroke, are refuges for migratory birds. Each year, thousands of curlews, sandpipers, tattlers and others break their journey from the Northern Hemisphere to rest on the tidal flats of the islands' sheltered western sides. They join a group of permanent residents which includes two large and magnificent ocean-dwelling birds of prey.

The White-bellied Sea-Eagle splashes into the sea to take surface fish and also dines on whatever it can find along the tideline. The Osprey, rare in most parts of the world, is a long-winged diver, which carries fish back to its bulky stick nest securely grasped in its powerful, spiky-soled feet. I have spent many enjoyable hours photographing birds on the ocean's edge. If you care to do so, be aware that your life will be dominated by the tides and by the length of your lens — preferably 500 millimetres or longer.

THE SANDS OF STRADBROKE ISLAND

A BAND OF MIGRATORY WADERS RESTS, EACH BIRD BRACED AGAINST THE SEAWIND ON ONE SLENDER LEG

THE GOLD COAST, ONE OF THE WORLD'S BEST-KNOWN SEASIDE RESORT AREAS

LOOKING NORTHWARDS ALONG THE GOLD COAST'S FAMOUS BEACHES

Walking the length of a Gold Coast beach is a fascinating experience. I am only one of many people addicted to the delights of strolling the sand, enjoying the delights of sea, sunshine and cooling breeze. I particularly enjoy watching the ever-changing panorama of Coast residents, day visitors and overseas tourists, every single one of them intent on getting the most out of his, or her, very own Gold Coast experience. As I beach-walk, the sea lies on one hand, and on the other are restaurants, shopping malls, boutiques and amusement venues, all of them dedicated to making any day, or night, at "The Coast" a memorable one.

GOLD COAST TWILIGHT

I have come to relish the Gold Coast's ever-changing seascapes, the long golden beaches, and the easy access inland to rugged, rainforest-covered mountains and sheltered rural valleys where ways of life hardly seem to have changed for decades. I am especially fond of the moments at dawn and at sunset when the sometimes hectic pace of Gold Coast life slows and reflections shimmer like opals across calm waters.

THE BROADWATER, MAIN BEACH

HOUSES CROWD THE CLIFFS NEAR SYDNEY

NEW SOUTH WALES

SEABIRDS RISING AS ONE

A fair proportion of Australia's population lives along the New South Wales seacoast. The marine life of that sea coast is quite unlike that of Queensland, for the interaction between subtropical and temperate waters, and the substitution of rocky for coral reefs, give rise to a vastly different set of living conditions.

New South Wales' coastal scenery varies spectacularly from the long, gentle sandy arcs of the northern coast and the sweeping and splendid southern beaches to the stark cliffs and towering headlands of the central coast and Sydney surrounds.

Nowhere else in Australia do so many people live perched on top of steep and formidable cliffs than near Sydney, Australia's premier seaside city. These "cliff-hangers" seem to symbolise the desire of most Sydneysiders to live as near the ocean as possible. Magnificent Port Jackson boasts two world-famous man-made sea-icons, the shell-like Opera House and the massive Sydney Harbour Bridge. Each Boxing Day, the start of the biggest ocean event of all, the Sydney to Hobart Yacht Race, brings a festival of shipping, great and small, in "our Harbour".

Sydney sets the fashion, but every coastal town celebrates the ocean in its own way.

The photos that follow show some of the memorable and eye-catching aspects of this great State's coastline.

BYRON BAY LIGHTHOUSE IS SITUATED ON AUSTRALIA'S MOST EASTERLY HEADLAND

VIEW SOUTH FROM BYRON BAY DOWN TALLOW BEACH TOWARDS BROKEN HEAD

SUNBATHING AT BYRON BAY

Each evening, the lighthouse on Cape Byron, Australia's most easterly point, casts its powerful glow over 26 kilometres into the inky blackness of the Pacific Ocean. The view from the lighthouse is magnificent by night or day, particularly the vista looking south down Tallow Beach towards Broken Head. Fifteen years ago I dived the Julian Rocks Aquatic Nature Reserve every weekend that weather permitted (and on some days when no sensible diver would have donned a mask). I spent many, many entranced hours below the surface, watching fish and invertebrates from the warmer north mingle with marine creatures from cooler southern waters.

During the warmer months, the beaches around Byron Bay are filled with happy holidaymakers soaking up the sun. All the seaside sports are available – diving, fishing, sailing and powerboating – and hang-gliding buffs travel here from all over Australia to soar with the sea-eagles above the headland, finally swooping to land safely on Tallow Beach several hundred metres below.

YURAYGIR NATIONAL PARK

Near Grafton, Yuraygir National Park extends around 60 kilometres from Yamba to Red Rock. This is a great area for nature lovers, with extensive freshwater lakes and stretches of heathland which in springtime are glorious with wildflowers and full of eagerly feeding birds and insects. A series of nature trails and wetland boardwalks allows access to the area while protecting its fragile habitats. The beaches are typical of those in the Northern Rivers of New South Wales, long, gentle sweeps of crisp sand, bordering warm, clear water. This is a fishing paradise – for people, and for pelicans, ospreys, terns and other seabirds.

DIAMOND HEAD, CROWDY BAY NATIONAL PARK

THE MAGNIFICENT SWEEPING BEACH AT CROWDY BAY NATIONAL PARK

A WELL-CONCEALED, VERY LARGE DUSKY FLATHEAD

AN EMOTIONAL BUTTERFLY GURNARD FLASHES ITS FINS

Sand is one of Australia's national treasures and the shifting sandbanks of the northern New South Wales coast give the lie to the theory that all the most fascinating marine animals live around coral or rocky reefs. To view the life of a sandy seabed at its best, try diving at night. Intriguing fish include the huge Dusky Flathead and the delicate, fin-flashing Butterfly Gurnard. They share their world with sea pens, gobies, star gazers, sea stars, anemones, gudgeons and many more marvels, all living under or on the sand.

TOMAREE HEAD, TOMAREE NATIONAL PARK

Those who love catching fish know that the enchanted time when the first rays of the sun light a path across the water is the best time of day (especially if the fish are biting!).

Nelson Bay is a popular fishing and boating spot for the people of Sydney and its northern neighbour Newcastle. The small and interrupted Tomaree National Park is nearby. It is under siege from a pest plant, the bitou bush, but its bird life is remarkable and the beaches even support a colony of nesting Little Penguins, possibly the most northerly in eastern Australia.

DAWN AT TOMAREE NATIONAL PARK, NELSON BAY

A FLOTILLA OF PELICANS AT TUGGERAH LAKES

TERRIGAL BEACH ON THE CENTRAL COAST

BEACH FISHING AT THE ENTRANCE

The Australian Pelican, with its enormous bill, comical enquiring look and awkwardly splayed, webbed feet is a popular bird. The colony resident at Tuggerah Lakes provides entertainment for human onlookers and a ready disposal service for unwanted fishy scraps. The New South Wales Central Coast is a fast-growing area, which boasts centres such as The Entrance, Terrigal, Avoca Beach, Broken Bay and Gosford, while Bouddi National Park provides an additional attraction.

SUNRISE ON THE CENTRAL COAST

THE SKILLION, A LANDMARK NEAR TERRIGAL ON THE CENTRAL COAST

AVOCA BEACH

BLUE BAY AND TOOWOON BAY

Once the Central Coast was all but deserted during the week, but came alive each weekend, when visitors from Sydney and other centres of population arrived to relax in their seaside cottages. Today the permanent population is much larger, but there are still plenty of out-of-towners who regard time spent at Central Coast beaches as next best thing to a holiday in heaven.

MANLY IS ONE OF AUSTRALIA'S MOST POPULAR BEACHES

THE *ORIANA*, A HUGE PASSENGER LINER, IN PORT JACKSON

A REPLICA OF THE FAMOUS *BOUNTY* BERTHED AT CIRCULAR QUAY

Sydney Harbour, as Port Jackson is usually known, is one of the world's great bodies of water and one of the most picturesque places on all Australia's coast. I have lived on it in warships, I have dived in it, I have photographed its marine life and flown over it, and I love it from its most intimate tiny coves to its huge and majestic Heads. I am sure most of Sydney's residents share my enjoyment of their Harbour and certainly they take every opportunity to come to close quarters with it. Boats of every size and shape ply its waters, including enormous cruise liners like the *Oriana* and old-time tall ships such as the replica of HMS *Bounty* shown above moored at Circular Quay.

THE CITY OF SYDNEY HAS A CLOSE RELATIONSHIP WITH PORT JACKSON, ONE OF THE WORLD'S GREAT HARBOURS

SYDNEY AQUARIUM, DARLING HARBOUR

THE SYDNEY 2000 OLYMPIC INFORMATION CENTRE, WITH HARBOURSIDE FESTIVAL MARKETPLACE IN THE BACKGROUND

THE SAFEST WAY TO TO SEE SYDNEY HARBOUR UNDER WATER
IS AT THE SYDNEY AQUARIUM, DARLING HARBOUR

Darling Harbour is one of Sydney's major attractions, offering Harbourside Festival Marketplace, fine restaurants and cafes, an Exhibition Centre and, a short stroll away, the Powerhouse Museum. Sydney Aquarium allows people of all ages and physical conditions to discover the marine life of Port Jackson and the Australian coasts. The fine exhibits feature sharks, stingrays, seals and a host of other ocean-dwellers and transport observers to a variety of undersea locations without donning wetsuits, or even getting their feet wet.

THE BLACK-BANDED SEA PERCH IS COMMON AROUND SYDNEY HEADS

THIS DELIGHTFUL FISH IS KNOWN AS AN OLD WIFE

THE FIRE BRICK SEASTAR IS ONE OF THE LARGEST SEASTARS FOUND IN SOUTHERN WATERS

THE STRIPY FORMS LARGE SCHOOLS AND IS COMMON IN HARBOUR WATERS

NANNYGAI, OR REDFISH, ARE COMMON IN THE DEEPER WATERS AROUND SYDNEY HEADS

THE VERMILION BISCUIT STAR IS A BRILLIANT PORT JACKSON RESIDENT

I had my first taste of diving on Australia's east coast in Port Jackson almost 25 years ago. In these waters, I was to discover that the deeper I went the more profuse the marine life became (this is not the case further north on the Great Barrier Reef, where life forms are most prolific in shallow water). Of course, light from the surface diminishes rapidly with increasing depth, but in the photographs on these pages that problem has been overcome by the use of electronic flash, which reveals vivid colours which would be unseen by the naked eye.

SYDNEY OPERA HOUSE AND SYDNEY HARBOUR BRIDGE: AUSTRALIA'S MOST FAMOUS MARINE ICONS

For many people, Sydney Harbour Bridge and Sydney Opera House are symbols of Australia, one spanning a harbour, one rising on its shores. The Bridge was opened in 1932 and spans the half-kilometre between Dawes Point, at The Rocks, and North Sydney's Milson Point. The highest part of the arch rises 134 metres above the water and the structure may carry more than 15 000 vehicles per hour in peak traffic. Designed by Jorn Utzon, the Opera House took 14 years to build and was opened in 1973. It has four theatres and provides a fine venue for concerts, opera, plays and recitals.

The splendour of these icons is best captured on film just after the sun has set, when the sky is glorious with afterglow.

THE SYDNEY TO HOBART YACHT RACE IS AN ANNUAL EVENT WHICH FILLS THE HARBOUR WITH ACTION AND COLOUR

In many parts of the world, sailing is a sport for the very rich, but in Australia there is a sailing craft to suit any pocket and every level of expertise. Of course the glamorous "maxis", majestic stars of the Sydney to Hobart and other ocean races, cost the earth to build, maintain and sail, but at the other end of the scale there are any number of modest, but exciting, vessels.

There is a wonderful camaraderie that links mates who have spent a day on the water together and who return to shore, sunburned, salt-sprayed and cheerfully exhausted, to share a few cold drinks and memories of a great day's sailing.

LOOKING ACROSS THE CLIFFS OF THE GAP TO WATSONS BAY AND SYDNEY HARBOUR

BONDI BEACH, FAMED AS "ONE THOUSAND METRES OF GOLDEN SAND"

Bondi, closest ocean beach to the city of Sydney, is one of the line of great surfing beaches that stretches south to Botany Bay and includes Bronte, Tamarama, Coogee and Maroubra. Its Surf Lifesaving Club, one of Australia's oldest, was founded in 1906. Annually, Bondi serves as the finish point for the City to Surf Fun Run. Originally this golden stretch of sand was called "Bundi"; today it is so famous that its name is recognised internationally even without the further identification "Beach" tacked onto it.

GALLANT LIFESAVERS BATTLE CHOPPY SEAS

SURF HERO

ACTION ON LAND AT A SURF LIFESAVING CARNIVAL

Surfboard riding was introduced to Australia by Hawaii's Duke Kahanamoku, at Freshwater Beach in 1914. Eleven years beforehand, and just to the south, Australia's first Surf Life Saving Service had appeared at Manly, using an old fishing boat to brave the waves and drag drowners from the deep. The muscular, tanned, awesomely fit men and women who patrol Australia's metropolitan beaches save lives and form a tourist attraction in their own right. I like to look at them and think (of the men, anyway) that they bear a distinct resemblance to me in my youth.

119

GLADIATORS READY TO BATTLE THE SURF TO SAVE LIVES

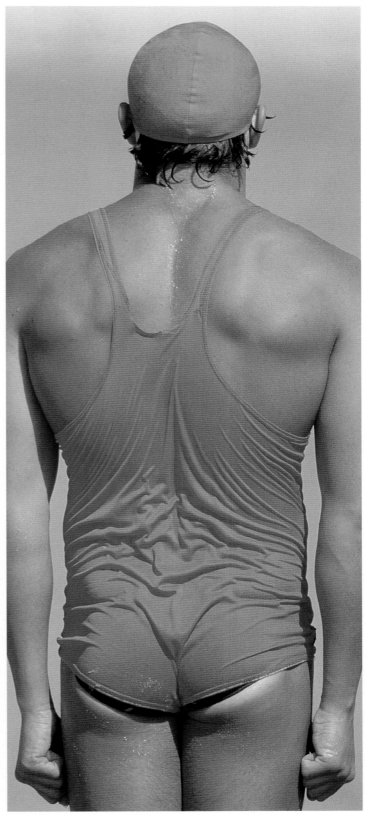

KNIGHT IN BRONZED ARMOUR

BALLS PYRAMID RISES 552 METRES FROM THE SEA SOUTHEAST OF LORD HOWE ISLAND

THE ADMIRALTY ISLES, HOME TO MANY BREEDING SEA BIRDS AND A MAGNIFICENT DIVING SITE

A RED-TAILED TROPICBIRD WITH ITS CHICK

The Lord Howe group of islands has been a World Heritage Area since 1982. When I landed on Lord Howe, I was enchanted by the sight of Red-tailed Tropicbirds soaring in the seawind, trailing their scarlet tail-ribbons. Lord Howe has a large colony of these exquisite seabirds. I was also enchanted by the prospect of diving the world's most southerly coral reef, where fish and a diversity of other marine life abound. I was *not* tempted to climb Balls Pyramid, a massive hunk of rock shoved above the waves by undersea eruptions around seven million years ago.

LORD HOWE ISLAND, A WORLD WHERE TIME CAN STAND STILL

FISH FEEDING AT NEDS BEACH

GIANT KINGFISH AND TREVALLY PATROL THE SHALLOWS WAITING FOR HANDOUTS

Neds Beach, one of Lord Howe Island's beautiful places, introduced me to a wonderful interaction between people and fish. For around 15 years, locals have been hand-feeding fish in the shallows and every afternoon at five o'clock tailor, bream, parrotfish, pop-eyed mullet, trevally and other species weave through the crystal shallows, impatiently waiting for the chance to join in a spectacular feeding frenzy. Nowhere else have I been able to snorkel alongside giant kingfish, some almost two metres long, and reach out and touch them, while they ignored me, their whole attention focused on getting their share of the goodies.

THE LIONFISH, ONE OF THE OCEAN'S MOST BEAUTIFUL CREATURES

Diving at Lord Howe can be a disorienting experience. In one place the sea floor resembles the vista I am used to in northern New South Wales, in another, not too far away, the coral is so profuse I feel I have been suddenly transported to the Great Barrier Reef. However, Lord Howe has its own unique marine fauna: a number of invertebrates and several species of fish, including an anemone fish and the Lord Howe Island Coral Fish, are found nowhere else. It takes extremely bad weather to spoil diving at Lord Howe.

CONSPICUOUS ANGELFISH

DOUBLE-HEADED WRASSE

THREE-BANDED CORALFISH

127

GORGONIAN CORALS AND FEATHER STARS

PAINTED CRAY, COMMON AT LORD HOWE

SLIPPER LOBSTER, ALSO CALLED A SHOVEL-NOSED CRAY

THE STRIPED BOARFISH, A SPECIES NOT FOUND IN MAINLAND WATERS

Every now and then I have an underwater experience that makes my heart race with excitement, and encountering this Striped Boarfish while diving at Lord Howe was one such occasion. In mainland water I had swum with the Giant and the Long-snouted Boarfish, but thought that my chances of ever pulling the Striped Boarfish into focus were slim. I discovered that this large species swims in groups of five or six, moving slowly across the sea floor, poking its long snout into the nooks and crannies of rocks and corals in search of tasty hidden invertebrates.

A VIEW ACROSS FLAGSTAFF POINT TO WOLLONGONG

South of Sydney is Royal National Park and south of that is the city of Wollongong, confined between the sea and the sandstone edges of a forested escarpment. Once, this area carried luxuriant rainforest, which attracted timber-getters. Today, coal-rich Wollongong is a centre of industry but also has a pleasant sea-face, with a harbour full of fishing boats and pleasure craft. In fact, the city's name is said to come from an Aboriginal term for "sound of the sea". Beyond Wollongong is the charming town of Kiama, whose name is also attributed to an Aboriginal term, in this case "where the sea makes a noise".

POINT PERPENDICULAR, AT THE NORTHERN ENTRANCE TO JERVIS BAY

ONE OF THE AREA'S SPLENDID UNSPOILED BEACHES

HONEYMOON BAY, A SMALL COVE WITHIN JERVIS BAY

ST GEORGES HEAD

Jervis Bay, with its rocky headlands and aquamarine bays, is in one of Australia's most magnificent coastal areas and I was very lucky to be drafted there in the Navy almost 30 years ago. I spent nine years exploring the deepwater reefs of the area, one of the first fortunate few to dive there.

Both the headlands which guard the bay have limited access and the region supports wonderful woodlands and heathlands, which are home to a wide range of birds. The southern peninsula is a National Park, the northern one a military bombing range – quite a contrast!

MAORI WRASSE, A SCHOOL OF BUTTERFLY PERCH AND A SEA FLOOR PAINTED WITH BRIGHTLY COLOURED SPONGES – A TYPICAL SCENE IN THE DEEP WATERS OF JERVIS BAY

THE BLUE-TIPPED LONGFIN, A SPECTACULAR DENIZEN OF ROCKY REEFS AROUND JERVIS BAY

The marine life around Jervis Bay is particularly plentiful below 30 metres: the best dive sites are situated outside the bay, north or south along the steep cliffs. In one area, off Stoney Creek, the sea floor drops over a series of steps to 65 metres. I have dived a great many times on the lower ledges, where the marine life is sensational, with giant gorgonian sea fans, huge sponges and large schools of sea perch. In those early days, giant crayfish crawled the bottom and we were frequently circled by schools of kingfish. Whale sharks, sunfish and humpback whales all pass along the cliffs following the ocean currents either north or south.

The Blue-tipped Longfin is by far the most spectacular rocky reef fish found in the area. It is a lurking carnivore with a comparatively small home territory range. Although it is a shy fish, I became quite familiar with a number of individuals and I visited the one above over a period of five years. During the courting season longfins become very aggressive and showy, males and females displaying by puffing their throats and extending and quivering their long flowing fins.

Jervis Bay is, without doubt, an area which should be declared a World Heritage National Park.

BANDED SEA PERCH

RED ROCKCOD

HALF-BANDED PERCH

TURA BEACH AND MERIMBULA

PART OF THE FISHING FLEET AT EDEN, MAIN PORT FOR THE SOUTH COAST OF NEW SOUTH WALES

Ulladulla, Batemans Bay, Merimbula and Eden are delightful towns along the sparsely populated southern coast of New South Wales. Eden is the main port for the area. It is situated on a promontory which splits picturesque Twofold Bay in two. The site was originally chosen as a base for whaling and the harbour continues business shipping timber. Today the primary marine industry is fishing, and each year the fleet based at Snug Cove catches over 5000 tones of tuna, snapper, flathead, redfish, salmon and abalone, destined for the fish enthusiasts of Sydney and Melbourne.

THE SEA-CLIFFS AT EDEN, JUST PART OF THE SPECTACULAR "SAPPHIRE COAST"

VICTORIA

Victoria holds many memories for me. My first taste of salt water was at Rosebud, on the Mornington Peninsula, and I remember fondly many outings to the piers of Port Phillip Bay where I caught, with great enthusiasm, toadfish after toadfish.

The sea coast of Victoria, from Mallacoota in the east to Portland in the west, offers many gifts to photographers. The light in these southern latitudes is quite remarkable – soft, clear and penetrating. The effects of that light on a coast whose aspects vary from stark and rugged rocky cliffs to superb stretches of shining sand, from quiet estuaries full of bird life to popular western surfing beaches, guarantees exceptional photographs.

On the eastern side of Melbourne, the country around Lakes Entrance is renowned for peace and scenic beauty. To the west, the Great Ocean Road from Geelong to Port Fairy is one of Australia's most popular drives and justly so, for it offers splendid mountain and coastal scenery for almost 300 kilometres. Right around the coastline, fine National Parks offer protection not only to animals but also to unique heathlands, precious dune vegetation and even majestic stands of tall forest. Little Penguins, Australian Fur-seals, and a host of other easily viewed and fascinating saltwater creatures make Victoria a memorable State for the marine nature lover.

STEPS TO DISCOVERY

141

WILSONS PROMONTORY

Wilsons Promontory National Park features the southernmost point on the Australian mainland. This rugged and scenic Park covers around 50 000 hectares and is bordered by varying seascapes: there are sheltered bays to the east of the promontory and surf-swept bays to its west. The Promontory is a haven for those who wish to relax, and for other hardy souls who delight in meeting the challenges of bushwalking and enjoy looking at nature's beauty along their chosen trails.

COMMON WOMBAT IN THE DUNES, WILSONS PROMONTORY

I make every effort to visit places like Wilsons Promontory on weekdays, preferably during the winter when few people visit. At these times I make many encounters like the one recorded above, which gave me quite a surprise. I had seen Dingos and kangaroos on the beach, but never a wombat. This delightful chocolate-brown Common Wombat was waddling through the sand dunes, so intent on grubbing for tasty grass roots that it was oblivious to my presence.

POINT GRANT, PHILLIP ISLAND

Phillip Island, with its scenic Point Grant, its easily viewed Australian Fur-seal colonies and its charming and world-famous parade of Little Penguins, may well be the most popular tourist attraction in Victoria.

The island's wildlife is protected and much loved. Each evening when the Little Penguins are breeding, visitors flock to watch them leave the sea and "parade" to feed their chicks, or to relieve mates keeping eggs warm in nest burrows in the sand dunes. In the 1800s, sealers decimated the Australian Fur-seal colony, so that by 1860 there were only a few of these sea-living mammals breeding on Seal Rocks, just off the western end of the island. Today, seal numbers are recovering.

CAPE WOOLAMAI, PHILLIP ISLAND. PHOTO: PHILLIP HAYSON

PARADING PENGUINS

Little Penguins mate for life. Each springtime a pair lay two eggs in a nest they have excavated in the sand under a bush or rock. The parents take turns to brood the two eggs, and when finally the chicks hatch they go to sea each dawn to catch fish. Each evening, they return to the beach and waddle to their nest to feed their hungry offspring. At Phillip Island, and other places on Australia's southern coast, people gather to watch penguins "parade" from the sea to perform their parenting duties.

A SQUID SWOOPS THROUGH THE INKY BLACKNESS OF THE NIGHT SEA

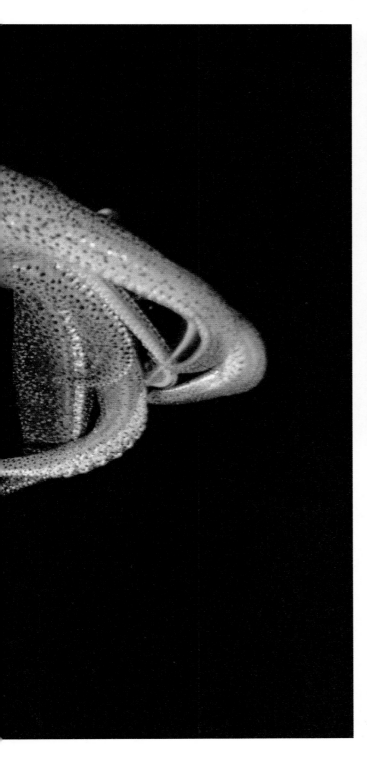

THE BIG-BELLIED SEAHORSE LIVES IN PORT PHILLIP BAY

Port Phillip Bay has a number of piers, giving easy access to a sea in which the night-time marine life is immeasurably more interesting than the daytime human on-pier life could possibly be. Apart from the chilly southerly wind that invariably bites as I gear up, piers have provided me with some great diving experiences. It was while diving from one of Port Phillip Bay's piers that I managed to capture my first squid full-frame. Squid mainly feed at night and this one was attracted to my underwater lights. Like all squid, it moved at alarming speed, and I am not quite sure whether getting this one in focus was a matter of good judgement or simply of good luck on my part.

LOOKING EASTWARD ACROSS POINT NEPEAN DOWN MORNINGTON PENINSULA

A VIEW FROM PORT PHILLIP BAY ACROSS THE PENINSULA TO THE SOUTHERN OCEAN

It was at Rosebud Beach that as a child I first wet my feet in salt water. I have strong early memories of the Mornington Peninsula, a beautiful, if windswept, part of Australia, where Portsea, Sorrento, Blairgowrie, Rosebud, Dromana and Mornington are among the State's most popular holiday destinations. Unless you are lucky enough to fly over the peninsula, the best view of it is from the famous Arthurs Seat, a hill climbed by navigator Matthew Flinders on 27 April 1802. One of the advantages of holidaying on the Mornington Peninsula is that it is double-sided. It is possible to enjoy the rugged eastern sea coast when fine weather and gentle winds allow, then, when a "blow" is imminent, transfer family picnics, windsurfing, fishing and sailing to the quieter waters of Port Phillip Bay.

TWILIGHT, MORNINGTON PENINSULA, ON THE EASTERN SIDE OF PORT PHILLIP BAY

BRIGHTON BATHING BOXES FROM THE AIR

The bathing boxes at Brighton Beach are the pride and joy of owners who, every weekend, take up their privileged vantage points and enjoy the envious glances of ordinary beach-goers. These brightly painted little buildings appear to be a remnant of British influence on Australian culture, but they are much-loved icons of Melbourne's seafront and there would be few locals – or visitors to Victoria's capital – who did not sooner or later wander along the golden sand and admire the rainbow-coloured line-up.

JUST PLAYING – WE HOPE! BRIGHTON BATHING BOXES, PORT PHILLIP BAY

MELBOURNE SEEN THROUGH MASTS FROM ST KILDA PIER

FRIENDS AT SUNSET, ST KILDA PIER

"Melbourne a *seaside* city?" many Australians would ask in amazement. However, this gracious city stands on Port Phillip Bay, largest such indentation in the continent's coastline, and Melburnians love their Bay. To see Melbourne's multicultural citizens at their most delightful, visit St Kilda Pier on a sunny weekend. Dressed to catch the eye, people of all ages and origins stroll the Pier like a flock of exotic birds, ruffling their bright feathers, preening each other, flirting and indulging in courtship rituals.

WILLIAMSTOWN

Since British navigator Matthew Flinders steered the *Investigator* into Port Phillip Bay in 1800, vessels of all sorts have made use of this sheltered water. The *Polly Woodside*, a three-masted barque and the star of Melbourne's maritime museum, commemorates the days of tall sailing ships. She was built in 1885, around 30 years after the discovery of gold made Victoria a rich and well-populated State and turned Melbourne into a premier port.

THE *POLLY WOODSIDE*, A POPULAR MARITIME TOURIST ATTRACTION

CORIO BAY, GEELONG

FISHING BOATS MOORED IN CORIO BAY, GEELONG

Geelong, established on scenic Corio Bay in 1836, is just over 70 kilometres southwest from Melbourne. Today Victoria's second-largest city, in the nineteenth century Geelong exported wool and other produce from the rich Western District, as well as serving as nearest port to the goldfields. This beautiful city values its maritime history and displays it proudly. It also has a busy industrial waterfront, an active fishing fleet and a multitude of sailing craft, in which locals take to the water at every opportunity. Geelong guards the eastern end of one of Australia's great coastline experiences, Victoria's Great Ocean Road.

FORT QUEENSCLIFF, THE AUSTRALIAN ARMY'S OFFICER-TRAINING CENTRE

THE OZONE HOTEL, QUEENSCLIFF

Queenscliff stands on the Bellarine Peninsula, the western landmass guarding the entrance to Port Phillip Bay. Since the 1880s, when giant cannon were placed there in case of Russian invasion, the town has had a military air and indeed Fort Queenscliff is now home to the Australian Army Command Staff College.

SPLIT POINT LIGHTHOUSE, LOCALLY
KNOWN AS "THE WHITE LADY"

CAPE OTWAY LIGHTHOUSE, ERECTED AFTER
THE WRECK OF THE *CATARAQUI* IN 1845

POINT LONSDALE LIGHTHOUSE OVERLOOKS "THE RIP", THE TREACHEROUS
WATERS RUNNING THROUGH THE ENTRANCE TO PORT PHILLIP

One of my sea-heroes, Matthew Flinders was a man not easily moved by danger, but he commented that he had seldom seen a more fearful section of coastline than the stretch of Australia's southern margin we now call the Shipwreck Coast. Today, a number of lighthouses warn voyagers of the dangers of rips, currents, reefs and cliffs.

GOING TO THE BEACH, ONE OF AUSTRALIA'S MOST POPULAR ACTIVITIES

"We're going to the beach!" How many kids chant that in how many households during Australia's warmer months? Within sight of the ocean, the adults are left to carry the Esky, the beach umbrella, the 15+ sunscreen and food, while the kids rush ahead, kicking off thongs and flinging down towels. Once safely immersed in cold salt water, the triumphant front-runners forget their goosebumps in the joys of splashing the shuddering, shrieking late-comers, usually younger brothers or sisters whose shorter legs could not keep up in the headlong race across the sand.

OCEAN GROVE, TORQUAY, BELLS BEACH, LORNE AND MANY OTHER
BEACHES ARE POPULAR WITH THOSE WHO LOVE SAND, SUN AND SURF

EAGLE ROCK AT SPLIT POINT, NEAR AIREYS INLET

I am never lonely when I can hear the sea. Its messages echo from the depths where giant squid lead their secretive lives and from the saltwater roads travelled by great whales. They are full of the shrill voices of dolphins, the beating wings of seabirds, the grunts, groans and chirps of fish going about their underwater business. And the sea has its own voice – the endless rumble of water falling back on water, the grinding of stone wearing away stone, the silken hiss of spray, the murmur of waves retreating from sand.

Sometimes I talk to the sea, and who could say that the sea does not answer me?

LOOKING FROM AIREYS INLET TOWARDS FAIRHAVEN

THE INDENTED EDGE OF PORT CAMPBELL NATIONAL PARK

From Princetown to Peterborough, the Great
Ocean Road passes through Port Campbell
National Park, renowned for its spectacular and
rugged coastal landscape. Here limestone cliffs
drop sheer to the stormy Southern Ocean,
sculpted by waves and wind into stacks such as
the Twelve Apostles, London Bridge (now in
the process of demolition), Razorback Rock and
Muttonbird Island.

This 32-kilometre stretch of coast, where every
turn of the Great Ocean Road reveals new
scenic splendours, has seen some tragic
shipwrecks, most famous of which was the loss
of the three-masted *Loch Ard* in 1878.

TWILIGHT AT THE TWELVE APOSTLES

A SETTING SUN PAINTS THE SEA GOLD AND SILHOUETTES SOME OF THE TWELVE APOSTLES

MUTTONBIRD ISLAND

WALKWAYS ENABLE CLOSE VIEWING OF THE MANY GORGES AND HEADLANDS

The limestone and marine deposits of the Port Campbell National Park coastline are quite easily eroded by wave action. Caves undercut cliffs, then arches are formed and finally the arches collapse, leaving isolated stacks of rock. At one time London Bridge consisted of two arches, the landward one of which collapsed on 15 January 1990, just three days after I had walked across it and later taken the portrait shown opposite.

LONDON BRIDGE AFTER THE COLLAPSE OF ITS LANDWARD ARCH

LONDON BRIDGE'S LANDWARD ARCH, THREE DAYS BEFORE IT COLLAPSED

HOPKINS RIVER BOATHOUSES, RELICS OF WARRNAMBOOL'S MORE LEISURELY TIMES

FLAGSTAFF HILL MARITIME MUSEUM

Warrnambool is a delightful place to break a journey of discovery along the Great Ocean Road. Flagstaff Hill Maritime Village, with its lighthouse and fortifications dating to 1887, recreates the days of sail and displays historic vessels and shipwreck relics. The nineteenth-century Hopkins River Boathouse has been restored and displays historic vessels. Between June and October, whale-watchers can spot Southern Right Whales off this part of Australia's coastline.

GIANT KELP FORESTS IN MARIA ISLAND NATIONAL PARK

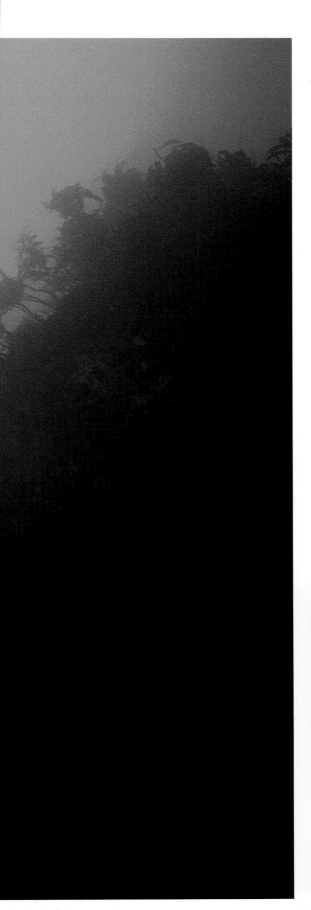

TASMANIA

Tasmania is unique amongst Australia's States because it is surrounded by sea. The southern end of Tasmania has some of the finest coastal scenery in the world, with islands, drowned valleys and picturesque bays and beaches. The beautiful State capital, Hobart, is set on the Derwent river and it seems that every one of its suburbs offers views of the sea.

Three of my most memorable sea experiences took place in Tasmania. One was gambolling with young sea-lions in the ocean off Ninth Island, Bass Strait. Another was to fly the wilderness that is the south coast late one afternoon, under a moody sky and above a stormy ocean.

The third, and the most memorable, was swimming in the giant kelp forests near Mistaken Cape, Maria Island National Park, off the central east coast of Tasmania. *Macrocystis* is a form of brown alga, whose long fronds are kept buoyant by gas-filled bladders. The undersea forest they form is filled with animals, from minute gastropod molluscs that graze the fronds, to octopus, sea urchins, sea dragons and a multitude of beautifully camouflaged small fishes that make the kelp fronds their roads and homes. To swim with seals in a cathedral of swaying golden kelp is a diver's idea of paradise.

BLADDERS GIVE BUOYANCY TO GIANT KELP

A YOUNG AUSTRALIAN FUR-SEAL BARREL-ROLLS TOWARDS THE CAMERA

SWIMMING WITH SEALS IS A MEMORABLE EXPERIENCE

I remember having a very bad attack of flu the day we visited Ninth Island. It was amazing how I forgot my aching limbs and sore head for the four hours we played with the young Australian Fur-seals that came to meet us. Fortunately, we were there during the breeding season, when the big bulls establish their island-based territories and are reluctant to leave their harems unattended. We had barely dropped anchor when a big-eyed, whiskered face popped out of the ocean beside the boat. I was overboard in minutes.

Talk about showing off! Seals are masters at it. A youngster would barrel-roll into the kelp, totally vanishing from view. Seconds later a head would poke out, then as suddenly disappear again. Then, with an explosion of bubbles, the pup would rush out from the kelp fronds straight at my face mask. A half-metre away, it would stop dead, open its mouth and blow a mouthful of air at me. With no warning it would undulate up to me, then pull at my flippers or pirouette on my head. What an experience!

HOBART, CITY ON THE DERWENT

ANOTHER VIEW OF HOBART'S SUBURBS

To arrive in Hobart from the mainland at night and to wake at sunrise the following day is to be shocked into thinking you caught the wrong plane and landed in another country. This is a charming and in many ways very Old World city, with delightful stone homes, historic docks and waterside warehouses, and gorgeous parks and gardens of cool-climate flowers. The twin attributes of towering Mount Wellington, especially in winter when it is snow-capped, and the magnificent Derwent River clearly set Hobart on its own in terms of sheer scenic splendour.

VICTORIA DOCK IS STEEPED IN HISTORY

The classic splendour of the early nineteenth century Georgian warehouses lining Hobart's immediate foreshore creates an immediate sense of history. One famous feature is Victoria Dock, which like all Hobart's splendid waterfront is especially festive after the gruelling Sydney to Hobart yacht race.

THE RUGGED COAST OF SOUTH WEST NATIONAL PARK

SOUTH WEST CAPE, AUSTRALIA'S MOST SOUTHERLY POINT

It is not particularly expensive to hire a light aircraft in Hobart and to head off to fly the wilderness coast of South West National Park. Though those more adventuresome will trek the wild coastal walking tracks, it is from the air that the true splendour of this magnificent part of the world can be fully appreciated.

There is Port Davey, with its massive Bathurst Harbour, and Payne Bay, then rugged South West Cape, Australia's southernmost landmass, Prion Bay, with its sweeping beach, coastal lagoon and estuarine heath, and the towering, often cloud-clad Precipitous Bluff. This is a World Heritage Area: when I am most stressed I float off to take refuge in it in my imagination, alone with the sea-eagles floating above the sea cliffs of this far southwestern wilderness.

THE WILD COASTS OF SOUTHERN TASMANIA OFFER SUPERB SCENERY

A LONE SAIL BOAT ON THE CALM WATERS OF BATHURST HARBOUR, A WILDERNESS BAY IN SOUTH WEST NATIONAL PARK

STORM CLOUDS, COORONG NATIONAL PARK

SOUTH AUSTRALIA

LIGHTHOUSE AND HISTORIC BUILDINGS AT QUEENS WHARF, PORT ADELAIDE

I spent my teens in Adelaide, on the eastern side of Gulf St Vincent, and the city and south coast beaches gave me my earliest introductions to the sea. Today, I love to explore South Australia's coastline, much of which is uninhabited and unspoiled and could well be classed as wilderness.

The photograph opposite expresses something I have always felt about South Australia's coasts – that the sky and the sea are co-stars in a continual drama. Like a perfectly matched pair of actors, their moods echo and play off each other, now moody and brooding, now bright, boisterous and brilliant, then within hours charming the audience with understated sensuality.

PROFESSIONAL CRAYFISHERMAN, ROBE

ROBE IS A WELL-KNOWN HOLIDAY RESORT AND HOME PORT FOR A PROFESSIONAL CRAYFISHING FLEET

Each September sees the opening of the crayfishing season on the southeast coast of South Australia. To dine on crays in the town of Robe, a centre for the industry, is one of the universe's great gourmet delights.

The port of Robe was proclaimed in 1847 and contains a number of fine examples of nineteenth century buildings. Today this holiday town is particularly popular with people who love to catch – and eat – fish.

SAILING THE BEACH AT PORT ELLIOT

BEACH FISHING, PORT ELLIOT

Victor Harbor, 83 kilometres south of Adelaide, was settled in 1837 to service whalers, then became a major port for the Murray River trade. It is now a leading tourist resort, where a favourite experience is to take a ride on the Cockle Train between Victor Harbor and Goolwa, near the mouth of the Murray. Another is the one-kilometre journey across a causeway from the port to Granite Island, a wildlife sanctuary noted for its Little Penguins. The journey can be made on a tram drawn by a massive and patient Clydesdale horse.

A HORSE-DRAWN TRAM CARRIES VISITORS FROM VICTOR HARBOR TO GRANITE ISLAND ACROSS A CAUSEWAY ESTABLISHED IN 1882

AN AERIAL VIEW OF GLENELG

A REPLICA OF HMS *BUFFALO* IS MOORED
IN PATAWALONGA BOAT HAVEN, GLENELG

On 28 December 1836, Captain Hindmarsh arrived at Holdfast Bay in HMS *Buffalo* with some 170 passengers and proclaimed the Province of South Australia. Today, a replica of the *Buffalo* lies near the original landing point at Glenelg, which also offers an historic jetty, colonial buildings, fine restaurants and all the pleasures of the seaside only ten kilometres from the centre of Adelaide city. The last remaining Adelaide tram route runs between the city centre and this busy and historic seaside suburb.

GLENELG JETTY

SUNSHOWER, CAPE DU COUEDIC, KANGAROO ISLAND

The most wonderful thing about photography is that it gives you an opportunity to capture special moments, then to keep them forever. The image above shows one of those occasions. We had booked into one of the lighthouse keeper's cottages at Cape Du Couedic, the southwestern point of Kangaroo Island. Having seen no one for three days we were revelling in solitude, visiting the Remarkable Rocks close by, watching fur-seals frolic in the cliff-base rock pools, exploring the giant limestone cave known as Admirals Arch and generally escaping into nature. On our last afternoon a storm blew in, emptied its load, then stopped as suddenly as it had begun. Within minutes the sun broke through, painting the Cape in shades of gold and putting the finishing touches to a marvellous experience.

CAPE DU COUEDIC LIGHTHOUSE

ADMIRALS ARCH, CAPE DU COUEDIC, FLINDERS CHASE NATIONAL PARK, KANGAROO ISLAND

SUNSET, CAPE DU COUEDIC

SEA-CLIFFS NEAR REMARKABLE ROCKS, KANGAROO ISLAND

REMARKABLE ROCKS

One of the challenges with visiting great monuments is viewing them at leisure without being disturbed by crowds of people. This is true for London's Westminster Abbey and the Roman Colosseum, and it is also true for nature's great works, such as Remarkable Rocks at Kilpatrick Point on Kangaroo Island. I try to visit places like this at sunrise, long before the crowds have left their beds. At that time of day, the light is superb and the great weathered boulders look like masterworks left for a moment by the sculptor creating them.

REMARKABLE ROCKS AT KILPATRICK POINT, FLINDERS CHASE NATIONAL PARK, KANGAROO ISLAND

AUSTRALIAN SEA-LION SCRATCHING ITS ITCHY NECK, SEAL BAY, KANGAROO ISLAND

AUSTRALIAN SEA-LION RESTING AFTER TIME SPENT AT SEA FISHING

AN ANXIOUS PUP GREETS ITS SEA-WEARY MOTHER

I was deeply impressed by the high level of sensitive and caring management shown by the South Australian National Parks and Wildlife Service at Seal Bay Conservation Park, Kangaroo Island. This is the only accessible breeding sea-lion colony on the Australian coast and watching the delightful pups and their protective mothers is a moving experience. Our Parks and Wildlife guide was not only passionate about the animals he was interpreting, but also cared about the human visitors. He set out to ensure that each person enjoyed the sea-lion colony emotionally, as well as understanding the biology of the animals.

SEASCAPE IN COFFIN BAY NATIONAL PARK

PORT AUGUSTA

My teenage years were filled with crabbing and snorkeling trips around the coasts of Coffin Bay National Park and Lincoln National Park, and on the wide tidal flats of Spencer Gulf and Gulf St Vincent. These sparsely populated coasts offer some of Australia's best opportunities for fishing, diving, sailing and generally escaping from the cares of the world.

PROUD OF THE CATCH

AN ASPECT OF A WHITE POINTER SHARK NO-ONE WANTS TO SEE

When I was a teenager in South Australia, my passion was spearfishing. In those days, television had not invaded every home, and as few people were interested in diving or surfing there was general ignorance about sharks. If I saw a shark, I simply regarded it as a big fish.

One day I was diving with a friend one kilometre from shore at Aldinga Reef, south of Adelaide. A four-metre-long White Pointer Shark swam towards us, grabbed our fish float and swallowed it in one gulp. The float was attached to my weight belt, which I quickly discarded. The shark circled, then disappeared into the blue, leaving us the memory of staring, icy eyes, a gaping mouth full of razor-edged teeth, and immense, controlled power.

We clutched each other like little kids for a while, then set off lickety-split for shore. If we had known then what we know now about White Pointers, we would have sprinted across the surface of the water. Within three years, White Pointers had made three attacks, one of them fatal, in the same area. Today, however, I have joined the ranks of admirers of the White Pointer, a savagely beautiful creature which is disappearing from the oceans. Only recently has the need to protect the species attracted worldwide support.

THE WHITE POINTER SHARK IS A MAGNIFICENT CREATURE

HEAD OF THE BIGHT, GREAT AUSTRALIAN BIGHT, SOUTH AUSTRALIA

WHALE-WATCHERS AT THE HEAD OF THE BIGHT

A SOUTHERN RIGHT WHALE TAIL-SLAPPING

Each spring, between June and September, Southern Right Whales migrate from the Antarctic to calve and mate along Australia's southern coastline. One of their favoured breeding destinations is a stretch of coast at the northern extremity of the Great Australian Bight known as the Head of the Bight. Here, in the comparatively calm waters off Twin Rocks, dozens of these enigmatic animals can be seen. Often they are so close to the cliff base that it is possible to look down upon them as they tail-slap, leap, roll and play with their calves. As an added bonus, the keen whale-watcher may also spot Humpback Whales in the area.

COASTAL DUNE, GREAT AUSTRALIAN BIGHT

SEA CLIFFS SHOW WHERE THE NULLARBOR PLAIN ENDS ALONG THE GREAT AUSTRALIAN BIGHT

The meeting of the Nullarbor Plain with the Great Australian Bight is marked by precipitous cliffs, some rising 90 metres above the Southern Ocean. The area once lay beneath the ocean and its limestone is honeycombed with caves. Climbing down through a "sinkhole" from the heat and glare of the surface into cool darkness is an awesome experience. I find it easy to believe that in the passages and caverns below I might come upon the mummified remains of a Thylacine, a "Tasmanian Tiger", such as lived on the Nullarbor only a few thousand years ago, when the area was marginally less arid, before the arrival of that more efficient predator the Dingo.

THE CLIFFS STRETCH FOR MANY KILOMETRES ALONG THE BIGHT

WESTERN AUSTRALIA

The coastline of Western Australia stretches for some 12 500 kilometres. The southern shores feature jutting granite headlands and sheltered, sandy bays. North of the "corner" formed by Capes Leeuwin and Naturaliste, the west coast commences with massive rocky outcrops, then continues as low limestone cliffs, sand beaches and dunes. Behind these barriers are heathlands, which every springtime flower into beauty.

My idea of a wonderful half-year would be to explore the rugged Kimberley coast during June, then drive south through Broome to reach Port Hedland by July. In that month, I would investigate the northwest coast, with its fauna-rich islands, then in August I would follow the coast southwards, taking in Ningaloo Marine Park, then Shark Bay (visiting the dolphins at Monkey Mia), and doing some diving (and searching for historic wrecks) as I follow the wildflower explosion to Perth. By late October, I would be on my way southwards, to adventure happily along the splendid coastline between Cape Leeuwin and Cape Arid National Park.

DOLPHINS ARE COMMON ON WESTERN AUSTRALIA'S SEA COAST

CAPE ARID, LIKE MANY PLACES ON WESTERN AUSTRALIA'S SOUTHERN COASTLINE, HAS SHINING SILVER SAND

CAPE LE GRAND NATIONAL PARK

Cape Arid National Park lies on the fringes of the Nullarbor Plain, while Cape Le Grand National Park is just east of the port of Esperance. These parks have spectacular scenery, bordered by white sand beaches and, in springtime and early summer, magnificent displays of wildflowers. This is a coastline for swimming and camping, bushwalking and photography.

CAPE LE GRAND NATIONAL PARK

Do you want to swim in your own private saltwater pool, whose sapphire water is so clear you can see individual grains of sand on the sea floor, where swimming costumes are not necessarily in fashion and you can walk the beach without meeting another soul? Try Cape Le Grand National Park, one of Australia's greatest coastal secrets, discovered so far by only a discriminating few.

WHALEBONE BEACH, FITZGERALD RIVER NATIONAL PARK, SOUTHWEST WESTERN AUSTRALIA

DIVING UNDER BUSSELTON JETTY

SCENES FROM LEEUWIN NATURALISTE NATIONAL PARK

Busselton is a port 230 kilometres south of Perth, on the shores of Geographe Bay (a coastal feature named for the ship of an early navigator in these waters). Its jetty, two kilometres in length, was once the longest in Australia, but was damaged by Cyclone Alby in 1978. Diving under and around the jetty is great fun, for the piles support a great and colourful variety of sea creatures. South of Busselton, Leeuwin Naturaliste National Park (named for two other historic ships) offers many scenic splendours.

A SHELTERED COVE ON ROTTNEST ISLAND

THE JOYS OF ROTTNEST ISLAND

Rottnest Island lies around 19 kilometres from Fremantle. It has for many years been a holiday haven and favoured fishing base for the residents of that port and Western Australia's capital, Perth. Of late years, "Rotto" has been increasingly discovered by "Eastern-Staters" and overseas tourists, who join the locals in all the Rottnest activities. These range from swimming, cycling, sailing, over-eating, and lazing around on the beach to watching Quokkas, those miniature wallabies which bound up, stick their cute little noses into your picnic lunch and demand immediate food and attention.

WESTWARD THE BLUE HORIZON

I have noticed that my friends born in Western Australia may roam widely over the world, even spend a few years "over East", but sooner or later they take their children back to the West coast and settle down happily. Often they make their homes within sight of the wonderful Indian Ocean, with easy access to one of the magnificent beaches which stretch from North Fremantle's Port Beach northwards to Mullaloo and from there to Sorrento and Yanchep.

REVELLING IN THE COOL INDIAN OCEAN ON ONE OF PERTH'S MAGNIFICENT BEACHES

SCARBOROUGH BEACH

Perth enjoys a Mediterranean climate, with long, hot, dry summer days, ideal for beach-going. A family expedition may well begin late in the afternoon, when the heat has gone from the day. Mum, Dad and kids and friends can swim, play a game of cricket or build sandcastles on the beach, then eat a picnic meal (perhaps from a beachfront kiosk) while the glowing sun sinks over the golden ocean and the lighthouse at Rottnest flashes like a firefly on the horizon.

COTTESLOE BEACH

ZUYTDORP CLIFFS, NEAR SHARK BAY

FRANÇOIS PERON NATIONAL PARK, SHARK BAY

230

DUGONGS ARE COMMON IN SHARK BAY: HERE A CALF RIDES ON ITS MOTHER'S BACK

THE DUGONG IS THE AUSTRALIAN REPRESENTATIVE OF A RARE AND VANISHING GROUP

Shark Bay is a huge, shallow area of water covering about 13 000 square kilometres. The Nanga and Peron Peninsulas and Dirk Hartog Island split the bay into two major sections, while underwater sand ridges and banks covered with seagrass, running more or less northwards, divide it into a series of basins. François Peron National Park, at the northern end of the Peron Peninsula, offers dramatic scenery and memorable wildlife. The waters of the bay are home to Dugong, gentle marine mammals which graze the seagrass. Dugongs belong to a group which includes manatees and sea-cows and is vanishing with human inroads into their aquatic homes. As the only marine member of the group the Dugong is particularly fascinating, and every effort should be made to preserve it and its habitat.

MONKEY MIA, PERON PENINSULA

Bottlenose Dolphins have been visiting the Shark Bay location known as Monkey Mia and meeting humans there since the 1960s. Today, Monkey Mia is one of the places the world's dolphin-watchers long to visit. Probably it is also famous in inter-dolphin communications about places to go and things to see. Certainly Monkey Mia's dolphins seem to enjoy "people-watching" as much as they relish the tasty fish sometimes handed to them (which occasionally a dolphin may choose to re-present to some lucky human as a gift).

DOLPHIN-WATCHING, MONKEY MIA

233

PEOPLE-WATCHING, MONKEY MIA

FEEDING THE SERGEANT MAJORS AT NINGALOO REEF

CORAL GARDENS AT NINGALOO REEF

WHALE SHARK

Ningaloo Marine Park extends for 260 kilometres along the coast of North-West Cape, from Amherst Point northeast to Bundegai Reef. In places the coral reefs are only around 100 metres offshore, and the area rivals the Great Barrier Reef for undersea riches. Three large marine species are regularly observed in Ningaloo waters – the Dugong, the Green Turtle and the awesome, but harmless, Whale Shark, which swims through the warm waters like some prehistoric monster, sucking tiny sea creatures into its gaping cavern of a mouth.

EIGHTY MILE BEACH AT LOW TIDE

AFTER CYCLONES, NORTHWEST BEACHES CAN BE PARADISES FOR SHELL COLLECTORS

I love to move around Australia's tropical coasts during the Wet season, when monsoonal storms arrive almost daily and there is always the chance of a really big blow. Cyclone Connie had just passed through when we arrived at Eighty Mile Beach, between Port Hedland and Broome. We had camped in the early hours of the morning, and at sunrise we were thrilled to see fantastic cloud patterns over the sea. I seized a camera and without pausing to perform any of the niceties of greeting the day, such as yawning, stretching, coffee-drinking or putting on clothes, took the shot opposite.

239

GANTHEAUME POINT, BROOME

Broome stands on Roebuck Bay and is a popular tourist and holiday town. Cable Beach, six kilometres from town, offers sapphire water and silver sand, which contrasts with the red sand typical of the pindan country inland. This popular beach ends at Gantheaume Point, whose colourful cliffs overlook rock in which 120 million years ago dinosaurs left their footprints. Today these are uncovered at low tide, providing a fascinating window into the past.

LUGGERS STRANDED ON THE MUD BY THE RETREATING TIDE, BROOME

In the early 1900s, Broome served as port for around 400 pearling luggers and produced around 80 per cent of the world's pearl shell. Most of the divers, who combed the seabed for shell dressed in cumbersome canvas suits and copper helmets, tethered to their luggers by air hoses, were from Asian countries. Many never returned to their families, but remained forever in foreign soil, in Broome's quiet cemetery.

FLOODED MCLARTY RANGE, TALBOT BAY, KIMBERLEY DIVISION

KING LEOPOLD RANGE, THE KIMBERLEY DIVISION

The seacoast of the Kimberley Division of Western Australia is often inaccessible except by sea and some of the most scenic areas are best appreciated by flying over them. This is particularly true of the marvellous patterns left on coastal mudflats by the outgoing tide, which in places such as King Sound rises and falls spectacularly. The wilderness rivers of the northern Kimberley Division, the tidal waterfalls at Talbot Bay and the wildlife and Aboriginal Wandjina figures of Drysdale River National Park are all difficult to reach but richly reward the effort.

PRINCE REGENT RIVER NATIONAL PARK

A MAGNIFICENT PART OF NATURE'S KINGDOM

Prince Regent River National Park covers around 640 000 hectares of Australia's most remote far northwestern corner. It is rugged sandstone and volcanic country, which contains a wealth of animal and plant species in an area classified as a World Biosphere Reserve. This is one of the world's few remaining true wild areas, which should be cherished and protected by all who value Earth's beauty and diversity.

THE SPLENDOUR OF WILDERNESS, PRINCE REGENT RIVER NATIONAL PARK

SUNRISE, DARWIN

NORTHERN TERRITORY

Much of the coastline of the Northern Territory may lack immediate appeal. In places there are lovely beaches, with clear, inviting water, but often mud takes the place of sand and the tideline is obscured by healthy stands of mangroves. The invitation of even the most sparkling sea is lessened by the suspicion that box jellies may be floating around (the number of divers' wetsuits worn by swimmers at Darwin's famed Casuarina Beach is probably higher than the number worn in an equivalent crowd in more southerly, chillier waters). However, the mudflats have their own animal population and the mangroves serve as nurseries for vast numbers of fish. Both environments have many visual charms and abound in striking subjects for the camera. Any place which offers Saltwater Crocodiles, exotic butterflies, kingfishers, egrets and sea-eagles, wallabies and mudskippers, as well as other remarkable creatures, is a favoured haunt of mine.

Aboriginal people have lived on this coast for many thousands of years, visited by South-East Asian seafarers, so it is rich in human history.

SUNSET, DARWIN

TWILIGHT, ARAFURA SEA

ANOTHER TWILIGHT SCENE

I learned early in my photographic career that the best time to expose colour film is around sunrise and sunset. I also learned that my favourite dawns and dusks are not necessarily those when the sky flares in brilliant scarlets and golds. I prefer more subtle tones, with pearly, light-filled mauves, pinks, roses, aquas and azures brought to shimmering life with tints of gold and silver, shaded with rich, jewel-toned rubies and amethysts. My advice to those who wish to capture such glories is – use a tripod, wait for the right moment to expose your film, then go for it! Every sunrise, every sunset is different and this particular combination of light, colour, reflections and cloud-shapes will never happen again.

A TREE OF LIFE OUTLINED IN SILT, KAKADU NATIONAL PARK

Mudflats are gorgeous in the hours when the sun's rays are low and the tide is going out. The retreating water flows along channels which from the air resemble veins on skin, or leafless branches on some enormous Tree of Life. Seen closer up, the mud is traced and tracked with the footprints and burrows of myriads of animals which make their living at various times of the cycle of the tides.

KAKADU MUDFLATS

MANGROVES DISPLAY THEIR AIR-LOVING ROOTS

Mangroves supplement their air supply through special roots which are exposed at low tide. At high tide, the tangle of roots becomes a haven for tiny fish fry, sheltering them from predators. Crabs and mudskippers also live by the tides, foraging across the grey, slippery ooze for tasty morsels when it is exposed, then retreating to burrows when the water rushes in to cover their feeding ground.

THE MUDSKIPPER ROWS ITSELF ACROSS THE MUD ON STUMPY "LEGS" OF PECTORAL FINS

A GOANNA ROAMS THE MUDFLATS AT LOW TIDE, LOOKING FOR TUCKER

A MUD CRAB THREATENINGLY BRANDISHES ITS CLAWS

MOUTH OF THE SOUTH ALLIGATOR RIVER

The rivers of northern Australia are influenced by the ocean for many kilometres from their mouths. During the Dry, they retreat into channels carved deep in their beds, while the Top End's animal life concentrates around them and on their isolated billabongs. During the Wet season, the rivers rush to the sea, flooding over the wetlands and plains. Saltwater crocodiles, turtles, fish, birds, frogs – all breed in a frenzy when the Wet dominates the coastal plains.

THE SOUTH ALLIGATOR RIVER ON A SPRING LOW TIDE AT THE HEIGHT OF THE DRY SEASON – A GOOD TIME TO SEE CROCODILES

OFFSHORE ISLANDS, PROPOSED LIMMEN GATE NATIONAL PARK

MANGROVE FORESTS IN THE PROPOSED LIMMEN NATIONAL PARK

The Aboriginal people discovered the natural riches of this part of Australia's northern coast a long time ago. Today, prawn trawlers and fishing vessels harvest the riches of the Gulf of Carpentaria, and the mangrove forests and mudflats of places such as the proposed Limmen Gate National Park are attracting nature lovers and adventurers in increasing numbers. These areas are particularly important as feeding and resting places for migrating birds from the Northern Hemisphere.

THE SEA PROVIDES PLEASURE, KNOWLEDGE AND ENCOUNTERS FOR ALL

A PLEA FOR SEA

The sea was the cradle of life. Today, it continues to contribute enormous amounts of its substance to the water cycle which makes life on Earth possible. It is full of plants and animals which humans find useful and edible, it carries shipping, adjusts the severities of climate and is of immense practical use to humanity. The sea soothes and inspires human emotions, moods and feelings. It is a thing of beauty in all its aspects and in its waters shelter creatures of wonder such as whales and dolphins.

In return for the sea's bounty, humans pour wastes into its water, poison its creatures, plunder its richness to fertilise their fields, use some of its most magnificent denizens to feed their domestic pets, spill oil to clog its surface and shores ... the list goes on and on.

Let me make a plea for the sea, since, although it has a multitude of voices, it speaks no human tongue.

The sea was my first playground and many of its creatures have become my friends. In times of trouble and sickness of spirit, I have gone to the sea and it has never failed to hold me, comfort me and inspire me to face the challenges of my future.

It has brought me love, and on its shores and in its waters I have realised many times how fortunate I am to have found a partner whose passion for the sea equals my own.

As Australians, we owe so much to the ocean which surrounds our continent in beauty. As citizens of the world, we cannot afford to destroy our oceans. Let us cherish our sea.

GO SEE AUSTRALIA

Highway One will take the hopeful traveller around much of Australia's seacoast. As the map above shows, the discovery of beaches, headlands and splendid sea vistas can be broken by stopovers in seaside resorts and a marvellous variety of small and hospitable coastal towns.

Australia's coastal National Parks showcase some of the world's most exciting and scenic areas. Facilities are generally excellent and by observing at dawn and dusk the camper will see wildlife not visible at midday.

The wilder regions, such as Tasmania's southwest and the far northwest Kimberley, can be viewed comfortably from the air or, with rather more hardship but untold satisfaction, on foot. Just remember that season is important here – Tasmania is more comfortable for campers in summer, the far north of Australia more accessible in winter.

To adventure Australia's coasts, on the beach or underwater, is a wonderfully satisfying experience. Choose your adventure on the map above, then see Australia!

ONESPOT SEA PERCH

WITH THANKS

My father gave me my first sea-gift, a face mask and snorkel. That single gift inspired me to take a direction that has given me hundreds of experiences that have motivated me to share my discoveries. I thank my father for that gift and his long support in the development of my publishing career.

Igo Oak handed me my first camera when I was 16, while we were diving on a seagrass sea-floor off Kangaroo Island in South Australia. That single act of sharing, and his subsequent encouragement with my photography, have enabled me to develop tools and skills that have provided me with these images.

Dr David Pollard, Dr Peter Sanger, Peter Ogilvie, Reg Lipson, Barry Andrewartha, Neville Coleman, Walt Deas, Tom Byron, Dr John Paxton, Doctors Tony and Avrill Ayling and Isobel Bennett have all inspired, assisted, encouraged and given of themselves, particularly during my early sea-years. Each has taught me something new, whether it was how to find animals, make pictures, write, publish and go on further to communicate with the world – not just with pictures, but also with words. You are my heroes, and I thank you.

A number of photographs in this book represent significant adventures that I experienced at times when I was not carrying a camera and sincerely wished that I was. I thank Jiri Lochman for photographs on pages 258 and 233, Kelvin Aitken for pages 206 and 207, Richard Woldendorp for pages 212 and 213, Geoff Taylor for pages 231 and 237, Ian Morris for page 253 (centre and bottom), Gerhard Saueracker for page 220 and the top photograph on page 236, Clay Bryce for the bottom picture on page 236, Diana Calder/Stock Photos for page 146 and Mark Simmons for his spectacular Humpback Whale photographs used on the front cover and pages 66 to 69.

I would also like to thank my wife and partner, Jan Parish, and also Phillip Hayson for their considerable support with the photography and, finally, a special thanks to Pat Slater for her enthusiastic support with the development of the text in this book.

For the expert design, colour separations and print production I give thanks to my own staff at Steve Parish Publishing.

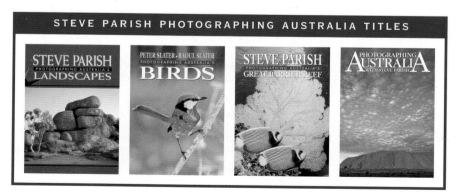

STEVE PARISH PHOTOGRAPHING AUSTRALIA TITLES

Steve Parish
PUBLISHING

© 1996 Copyright photography and text Steve Parish Publishing Pty Ltd

Published in Australia by Steve Parish Publishing Pty Ltd

PO Box 2160 Fortitude Valley BC Queensland 4006 Australia

PRINTED IN AUSTRALIA

National Library of Australia cataloguing in publication data:

Parish, Steve – Sea Australia

ISBN 1 875932 62 3

1. Photography – Australia

2. Title – Sea Australia